Bossing Without Lossing:

The Comedy and Wisdom of Team Leadership for Badass Managers

Dominika Gorecka

ISBN: 9798323604142

Imprint: Independently published

Table of Contents

Acknowledgements 5
Introduction 6
Chapter 1: Embracing Your Inner Badass 9
Chapter 2: Unleashing Your Inner Genius 12
Chapter 3: Mastering the Art of Business Meetings 16
Chapter 4: Navigating Conflict with Style and Grace 20
Chapter 5: The Art of Prepared Improvisation 24
Chapter 6: The Power of Rest and Renewal 28
Chapter 7: The Sherlock Holmes of Office Shenanigans 32
Chapter 8: The Art of Persuasion: Winning Hearts and Minds 36
Chapter 9: Navigating Sensitive Team Topics with Grace and Respect 40
Chapter 10: The Not-So-Standard Team Bonding: Tailored Fun for Your Unique Crew 44
Chapter 11: The Omniscient Manager: Balancing Insight and Autonomy 48
Chapter 12: Celebrating Diversity and Fostering Open Dialogue 52
Chapter 13: Aligning Team Goals with Executive Vision 56
Chapter 14: The Badge of Honour: Why Any Team Would Be Lucky to Have a Badass Manager 60
Chapter 15: From Bad to Badass: Turning a Rough Day into a Day of Triumph 64
Chapter 16: Unleashing the Badassery: Key Traits for Navigating Challenging Circumstances 68
Chapter 17: Leading Through Disagreement: Executing Difficult Tasks with Conviction and Collaboration 72
Chapter 18: Dispelling Myths: What a Badass Manager Isn't 76
Chapter 19: The Badass Manager vs. Michael Scott: Similarities and Differences 79
Chapter 20: The Joy of Having a Badass Manager 83
Chapter 21: The Unsung Hero: How Recognition Finds the Badass Manager 87

Chapter 22: Rebels with a Cause: How the Badass Manager Earns Respect through Rebellion 91
Chapter 23: Silent Champions: How the Badass Manager Supports Others Without Them Even Knowing..................95
Chapter 24: Embracing Unpopularity: Why the Badass Manager Isn't Always Liked by Others..................99
Chapter 25: Transformative Leadership: How the Badass Manager Turns Critics into Grateful Allies..................103
Chapter 26: Actions Speak Louder: How the Badass Manager Guides Talkers to Walkers 107
Chapter 27: The Illusion of Arrogance: Understanding the Badass Manager's True Nature..................111
Chapter 28: Provocative Leadership: How the Badass Manager Sparks Innovation Through Controversial Statements 115
Chapter 29: The Enigma of the Badass Manager: Embracing Mystery in Leadership..................119
Chapter 30: Zen and the Art of Badassery: The Manager's Path to Unwavering Resolve 123
Chapter 31: Embracing Curiosity: The Badass Manager's Quest for Originality 127
Chapter 32: Your Turn 131

Acknowledgements

To my parents, who always saw the potential in me even when I couldn't see it in myself, thank you for instilling in me the confidence to pursue my dreams and the resilience to overcome any obstacles in my path. Your unwavering faith in my abilities has been a guiding light, propelling me forward even in the darkest of times.

With all my love and gratitude,
Dominika

Introduction

Welcome to *Bossing Without Lossing: The Comedy and Wisdom of Team Leadership for Badass Managers* – the ultimate guide for those who aspire to be cool, brilliant, and wildly successful managers while still managing to keep their team members happy, achieve outstanding results, and maintain impeccable business relationships.

In the high-stakes game of leadership, being a badass manager isn't just about barking orders and counting wins. It's about mastering the delicate art of balancing authority with empathy, wit with wisdom, and ambition with authenticity.

In these pages, you'll embark on a journey filled with enlightenment and a few well-placed facepalms as we navigate the treacherous waters of modern leadership together. From mastering the art of the perfectly timed jokes to crafting strategic masterplans.

But fear not, dear reader, for this isn't your typical stuffy management manual. No, we're here to inject some much-needed levity into the often-serious world of leadership. So, prepare to hopefully laugh a tiny bit, learn, and maybe even snort your coffee as we dive into the wild and wonderful world of badass management.

Throughout these pages, you'll discover:

- The secrets to winning over your team with charm, charisma, and the occasional well-timed meme.
- How to navigate the rocky terrain of office politics with grace, tact, and just a touch of cunning.
- Strategies for motivating your team to achieve greatness while still allowing them the freedom to be their badass selves.
- The art of cultivating business relationships that are so strong, your competitors will wonder if you've secretly hired a team of mind readers.

So, grab your coffee (or your preferred beverage of choice), settle in, and get ready to unleash your inner badass manager. Because with a little comedy, a lot of wisdom, and the right attitude, there's no limit to what you can achieve. Let's boss without lossing, shall we?

Chapter 1: Embracing Your Inner Badass

Welcome, dear reader, to the first chapter of *Bossing Without Lossing: The Comedy and Wisdom of Team Leadership for Badass Managers*. In this chapter, we'll embark on a journey of self-discovery as we uncover what it truly means to embrace your inner badass and unleash your full potential as a manager.

But first, let's address the elephant in the room. What exactly is a badass manager? Is it someone who waltzes into the office wearing sunglasses and a leather jacket, exuding an aura of effortless cool? Well, maybe. But being a badass manager is about so much more than appearances.

At its core, being a badass manager is about embodying a set of principles and values that set you apart from the crowd. It's about having the courage to lead with authenticity, the wisdom to make tough decisions, and the humility to admit when you've made a mistake.

So, how do you tap into your inner badass? It all starts with embracing a few key principles:

1. **Confidence**: A badass manager exudes confidence in everything they do, from leading team meetings to tackling complex challenges. Confidence isn't about being arrogant or infallible; it's about believing in yourself and your ability to overcome obstacles with grace and poise.

2. **Authenticity**: Authenticity is the cornerstone of badassery. Be true to yourself, your values, and your vision for your team. Your team members will respect you more if they know you're genuine and sincere in your leadership approach.

3. **Empathy**: Contrary to popular belief, badass managers aren't heartless tyrants. They understand the importance of empathy and compassion in building strong, resilient teams. Take the time to listen to your team members, understand their concerns, and offer support when needed.

4. **Resilience**: Badass managers aren't deterred by setbacks or challenges; they thrive in the face of adversity. Cultivate resilience by learning from your failures, adapting to change, and maintaining a positive attitude even when the going gets tough.

5. **Humour**: Last but certainly not least, a healthy dose of humour can go a long way in the world of management. Don't be afraid to crack a joke or inject some levity into tense situations. Humour can break down barriers, foster camaraderie, and make the workplace a more enjoyable place to be.

As we delve deeper into the world of badass management, remember that being a badass isn't about conforming to a rigid set of rules or expectations. It's about finding your own unique leadership style and owning it with confidence and flair.

So, dear reader, are you ready to unleash your inner badass and embark on this journey of discovery with me? Buckle up, because we're just getting started.

Chapter 2: Unleashing Your Inner Genius

In this chapter, we'll delve deeper into the notion that behind every badass manager lies a secret genius waiting to be unleashed.

It's a common misconception that badass managers are all swagger and no substance. In reality, nothing could be further from the truth. Behind the cool exterior and witty banter lies a mind brimming with intelligence, creativity, and strategic prowess.

So, what sets a badass manager apart from the rest? It's their ability to harness their inner genius and use it to drive their team and organization toward success. Here's how they do it:

1. **Strategic Vision**: A badass manager possesses a keen strategic vision that allows them to see the bigger picture and anticipate future challenges and opportunities. They're not just focused on putting out fires; they're thinking several steps ahead, devising innovative

solutions, and charting a course toward long-term success.

2. **Problem-Solving Skills**: When faced with a complex problem or obstacle, a badass manager doesn't panic or shy away from the challenge. Instead, they roll up their sleeves, put their thinking caps on, and dive head-first into finding a solution. Their ability to think outside the box and approach problems from multiple angles often leads to ingenious solutions that others may have overlooked.

3. **Creativity**: Creativity is the lifeblood of badass management. Whether it's brainstorming new ideas, designing innovative processes, or crafting compelling presentations, badass managers aren't afraid to think outside the box and push the boundaries of what's possible. They're constantly challenging themselves and their team to break free from conventional thinking and explore new horizons.

4. **Emotional Intelligence**: Behind every badass manager's genius lies a deep well of emotional intelligence. They understand not only their own emotions but also those of their team members, enabling them to navigate interpersonal dynamics with finesse and empathy. This emotional intelligence allows them to build strong relationships, resolve conflicts, and inspire their team to greatness.

5. **Continuous Learning**: Perhaps the most defining characteristic of a badass manager's genius is their insatiable thirst for knowledge. They understand that the world is constantly evolving, and to stay ahead of the curve, they must be committed to lifelong learning and self-improvement. Whether it's devouring the latest management books, attending industry conferences, or seeking out mentorship opportunities, badass managers are always striving to expand their minds and enhance their skills.

In conclusion, behind every badass manager is a secret genius waiting to be unleashed. By tapping into their strategic vision, problem-solving skills, creativity, emotional intelligence, and commitment to continuous learning, badass managers have the power to transform their teams and organizations in ways that are nothing short of extraordinary.

Chapter 3: Mastering the Art of Business Meetings

In this chapter, we'll delve into the nitty-gritty of running efficient and effective business meetings with charm, charisma, wit, and your inner genius as a badass manager.

Business meetings – they're the necessary evil of corporate life. But fear not, dear reader, for with the right approach, you can transform even the most dreaded meetings into engaging and productive sessions that leave your team inspired and energized.

1. **Set Clear Objectives**: Before scheduling a meeting, clearly define the purpose and objectives. What do you hope to accomplish? What decisions need to be made? Setting clear objectives will help keep the meeting focused and on track.

2. **Prepare, Prepare, Prepare**: A badass manager never walks into a meeting unprepared. Take the time to gather all necessary materials, review relevant information, and

anticipate potential questions or objections. Your thorough preparation will not only impress your team but also ensure that the meeting runs smoothly.

3. **Start with a Bang**: The beginning of a meeting sets the tone for the entire session. Start with a captivating opening that grabs your team's attention and sets the stage for productive discussion. Whether it's a witty anecdote, an inspiring quote, or a thought-provoking question, make sure to kick things off with flair.

4. **Engage Your Audience**: A successful meeting is one where everyone feels engaged and involved. Encourage active participation by asking open-ended questions, soliciting input from quieter team members, and fostering a collaborative atmosphere where ideas can flow freely.

5. **Keep it Concise**: Time is precious, so make sure to keep your meetings concise and to the point. Stick to the agenda, avoid tangents, and cut through the fluff to get to the heart of the matter. Your team will thank you for respecting their time and keeping things efficient.

6. **Embrace Humour**: Injecting humour into your meetings can lighten the mood, break down barriers, and foster a sense of camaraderie among team members. Don't be afraid to crack a joke or share a funny story – just make sure it's appropriate for the context and audience.

7. **Facilitate Decision-Making**: A badass manager isn't afraid to make tough decisions, but they also know when to solicit input from their team. Facilitate decision-making by presenting options, soliciting feedback, and guiding the discussion toward a consensus. Your team will appreciate being part of the decision-making process and feel more invested in the outcomes.

8. **End on a High Note**: Just as a strong opening is crucial, so too is a memorable closing. End the meeting on a high note by summarizing key takeaways, outlining action items, and expressing gratitude to your team for their contributions. Leave everyone feeling inspired and motivated to tackle the tasks ahead.

By mastering the art of business meetings with charm, charisma, wit, and your inner genius as a badass manager, you'll not only run more efficient and effective meetings but also inspire greatness in your team and drive your organization toward success. So, go forth and conquer those meetings like the badass manager you are!

Chapter 4: Navigating Conflict with Style and Grace

Conflict – it's an inevitable part of any workplace, but it doesn't have to be a source of dread or discord. In this chapter, we'll explore how to navigate conflict with style and grace and your inner genius as a badass manager to foster resolution and strengthen team dynamics.

1. **Address Issues Head-On**: As a badass manager, you don't shy away from conflict – you tackle it head-on. When issues arise, address them promptly and directly, before they have a chance to escalate. Approach the situation with confidence and empathy, and strive to understand all perspectives involved.

2. **Listen Actively**: Effective conflict resolution begins with active listening. Take the time to hear out all parties involved, allowing them to express their thoughts, feelings, and concerns without interruption. Validate their

emotions and demonstrate empathy, even if you don't agree with their perspective.

3. **Find Common Ground**: Look for common ground and areas of agreement that can serve as a foundation for resolution. Encourage open dialogue and collaboration, and focus on finding mutually beneficial solutions that address the underlying issues at hand.

4. **Use Humour Wisely**: Humour can be a powerful tool for diffusing tension and breaking down barriers during conflict resolution. Use it wisely and with sensitivity, ensuring that it serves to lighten the mood and foster camaraderie rather than trivializing the seriousness of the situation.

5. **Maintain Composure**: As a badass manager, you maintain your composure even in the face of conflict. Stay calm, collected, and professional at all times, avoiding the temptation to react impulsively or emotionally. Your ability to stay level-headed will inspire confidence in your team and facilitate a more constructive resolution process.

6. **Focus on Solutions**: Shift the focus from blame and finger-pointing to finding solutions and moving forward. Encourage brainstorming and creativity, and explore alternative approaches that may not have been considered initially. By keeping the conversation focused on solutions, you'll create a more positive and productive atmosphere for resolution.

7. **Follow Up**: Conflict resolution doesn't end with a single conversation – it requires ongoing follow-up and support to ensure that issues are fully resolved and relationships are restored. Check in with all parties involved periodically to assess progress, address any lingering concerns, and reinforce the importance of maintaining open communication.

By navigating conflict with style and grace, using charm, charisma, wit, and your inner genius as a badass manager, you'll not only resolve issues more effectively but also strengthen trust, respect, and collaboration within your team. Conflict may be inevitable, but with the right approach, it can be an opportunity for growth, learning, and greater cohesion. So, embrace the challenge, and lead your team through conflict with confidence and poise.

Chapter 5: The Art of Prepared Improvisation

As a badass manager, you understand the importance of being prepared for any situation that may arise. But what sets you apart from the rest is your uncanny ability to improvise with style and finesse, seamlessly navigating unexpected challenges and opportunities with grace.

1. **Mastering Preparation**: Preparation is the cornerstone of success for any badass manager. You meticulously plan and anticipate every detail, ensuring that you're armed with the knowledge, resources, and strategies needed to tackle whatever comes your way. Your thorough preparation instills confidence in your team and sets the stage for success.

2. **Embracing Flexibility**: While preparation is crucial, you also recognize the importance of flexibility in a fast-paced and ever-changing environment. Life doesn't always go

according to plan, and as a badass manager, you're not afraid to adapt and pivot when circumstances demand it. You embrace change as an opportunity for growth and innovation, rather than a roadblock to success.

3. **Trusting Your Instincts**: As a master improviser, you trust your instincts and intuition to guide you through uncharted territory. You're not bound by rigid rules or conventional wisdom – instead, you rely on your gut feeling and creative intuition to make split-second decisions with confidence and conviction.

4. **Thinking on Your Feet**: In the heat of the moment, when the pressure is on and the stakes are high, you shine brightest. Your quick thinking and sharp wit enable you to think on your feet and devise ingenious solutions on the fly. Whether it's navigating a last-minute crisis or seizing a fleeting opportunity, you're always one step ahead, ready to take decisive action.

5. **Making it Look Effortless**: The true mark of a badass manager is making improvisation look effortless – so

effortless, in fact, that no one even notices you're doing it. Your seamless transitions, polished delivery, and flawless execution leave your team and colleagues in awe, wondering how you manage to pull it off with such ease.

6. **Learning from Experience**: Improvisation isn't just a skill – it's an art form that takes practice and experience to master. With each new challenge you face, you gain valuable insights and lessons learned that inform your future improvisational efforts. Every setback is an opportunity to grow stronger, more agile, and more adept at thinking on your feet.

7. **Inspiring Confidence**: Ultimately, the mark of a true badass manager is inspiring confidence in those around you. Your ability to improvise with style and grace, coupled with your unwavering composure and charisma, builds trust and reassurance in your team. They know that no matter what curveballs life throws their way, you'll be there to lead them through – again – with unwavering confidence and poise.

By mastering the art of prepared improvisation, you'll not only navigate the challenges of leadership with ease but also inspire greatness in your team and drive your organization toward success. So, embrace the unexpected, trust your instincts, and let your inner badass shine as you lead with style and finesse.

Chapter 6: The Power of Rest and Renewal

In the fast-paced world of business, there's often a relentless pressure to constantly be productive, to hustle non-stop, and to always be on top of your game. But as a badass manager, you understand the importance of balance and recognize that sometimes, the most productive thing your team can do is to take a break and rest their heads.

1. **Embracing Downtime**: Rest is not a luxury; it's a necessity for optimal performance. As a badass manager, you understand that pushing your team to work incessantly without breaks only leads to burnout and diminished productivity in the long run. Instead, you encourage your team to embrace downtime and prioritize self-care.

2. **Fostering Creativity**: Rest isn't just about physical rejuvenation – it's also about giving your mind the space it needs to recharge and replenish its creative reserves. When your team takes a break to faff around or indulge in

a bit of non-work-related banter, they're actually giving their brains the opportunity to wander, explore new ideas, and make unexpected connections that can lead to breakthrough innovations.

3. **Building Resilience**: Rest is a vital component of building resilience in your team. By allowing them the time and space they need to rest and recharge, you're helping them develop the mental and emotional fortitude to bounce back from setbacks and navigate challenges with grace and resilience.

4. **Enhancing Productivity**: Paradoxically, sometimes the most productive thing your team can do is to step away from their work and take a break. Regular breaks throughout the day can actually enhance productivity, improve focus, and boost creativity. By encouraging your team to rest and recharge, you're setting them up for greater success in the long run.

5. **Leading by Example**: As a badass manager, you lead by example when it comes to prioritizing rest and renewal.

You don't glorify overwork or sacrifice your well-being for the sake of productivity. Instead, you model healthy work-life balance and advocate for the importance of self-care, inspiring your team to do the same.

6. **Trusting Your Team**: Allowing your team the freedom to faff around and take breaks demonstrates a profound level of trust and respect. You trust that they understand their own needs and know when they need to step back and recharge. This trust fosters a sense of autonomy and empowerment, leading to greater job satisfaction and loyalty.

7. **Embracing Imperfection**: Finally, as a badass manager, you embrace imperfection and recognize that productivity isn't always linear. There will be times when your team needs to take a break, indulge in a bit of faffing around, or simply rest their heads. And that's okay. By letting go of the pressure to constantly be productive, you create a more relaxed and supportive work environment where your team can thrive.

By acknowledging the power of rest and renewal, you'll not only cultivate a happier, healthier, and more resilient team but also drive greater productivity and innovation in your organization. So, don't be afraid to let your team be unproductive from time to time – sometimes, a little faffing around is exactly what they need to come back stronger and more productive than ever.

Chapter 7: The Sherlock Holmes of Office Shenanigans

As a badass manager, you possess a superpower that sets you apart from the rest – the ability to discern truth from fiction with uncanny accuracy. In this chapter, we'll explore the art of reading between the lines, using your super insightful nature to navigate the murky waters of deception and uncover the truth.

1. **Cultivating Emotional Intelligence**: At the heart of your superpower lies a deep well of emotional intelligence. You have an innate ability to pick up on subtle cues – a fleeting expression, a shift in body language, a subtle change in tone – that reveal more than words ever could. By honing your emotional intelligence, you're able to read between the lines and discern the true motivations and intentions of those around you.

2. **Trusting Your Gut**: As a badass manager, you trust your gut instinct implicitly. You've learned to listen to that little

voice inside your head that whispers warnings and alerts you to potential deception. While evidence and facts are important, you know that sometimes your intuition can be the most reliable guide in discerning truth from falsehood.

3. **Asking the Right Questions**: When faced with a situation where truth is elusive, you know that asking the right questions is key. Your insightful nature enables you to probe beneath the surface, asking probing questions that reveal inconsistencies, contradictions, and hidden agendas. By digging deeper, you're able to uncover the truth that lies beneath the facade.

4. **Observing Non-Verbal Cues**: Words are just one part of the equation – you know that body language, facial expressions, and tone of voice can reveal volumes about a person's true thoughts and feelings. As a master observer, you pay attention to these non-verbal cues, using them to piece together the puzzle of human behaviour and uncover hidden truths.

5. **Creating a Safe Environment**: As a badass manager, you create a safe and supportive environment where honesty and transparency are valued above all else. Your team knows that they can come to you with their concerns and speak their minds without fear of reprisal. By fostering a culture of openness and trust, you make it easier for people to be honest and authentic in their interactions.

6. **Remaining Objective**: In your quest for truth, you remain steadfastly objective and impartial. You don't let personal biases or preconceived notions cloud your judgment – instead, you approach each situation with a clear and open mind, ready to evaluate the evidence and weigh the facts impartially.

7. **Handling Deception with Diplomacy**: When you uncover deception, you handle it with diplomacy and tact. You don't resort to accusation – instead, you use your insights to gently guide the conversation towards resolution and reconciliation. By approaching deception with empathy and understanding, you're able to maintain

trust and preserve relationships even in the face of conflict.

By mastering the art of reading between the lines, you'll not only uncover hidden truths and navigate deception with ease but also foster a culture of honesty, transparency, and trust within your team. So, trust your instincts, ask the right questions, and let your super insightful nature guide you as you uncover the truth and lead your team to greater heights of success.

Chapter 8: The Art of Persuasion: Winning Hearts and Minds

In the realm of leadership, the ability to change someone's mind – to sway opinions, shift perspectives, and win hearts and minds – is a formidable skill indeed. In this chapter, we'll explore how a badass manager can achieve their goals through the power of persuasion, earning the respect and admiration of others in the process.

1. **Understanding the Power of Influence**: As a badass manager, you understand that true influence isn't about coercion or manipulation – it's about inspiring others to see things from your perspective and willingly embrace your ideas. You recognize that persuasion is an art form that requires empathy, authenticity, and a genuine belief in the value of your message.

2. **Building Rapport and Trust**: Before you can hope to change someone's mind, you must first earn their trust

and respect. You invest time and effort in building genuine relationships with your team members and colleagues, listening to their concerns, understanding their perspectives, and demonstrating empathy and understanding. By building rapport and trust, you lay the foundation for effective persuasion.

3. **Crafting Compelling Arguments**: Persuasion begins with a compelling argument – a clear and convincing rationale for why your ideas are worth embracing. You take the time to gather evidence, marshal facts, and articulate your message with clarity and conviction. You anticipate potential objections and address them proactively, leaving no doubt in the minds of others about the validity of your ideas.

4. **Finding Common Ground**: Effective persuasion is often about finding common ground and appealing to shared values and interests. You look for points of agreement and areas of alignment between your goals and the goals of others, framing your message in a way that resonates with

their priorities and concerns. By highlighting shared objectives, you make it easier for others to see the value in your ideas and align themselves with your vision.

5. **Leveraging Social Proof**: People are more likely to be persuaded by ideas that are endorsed by others they respect and admire. As a badass manager, you leverage social proof to your advantage, enlisting the support of influential stakeholders, building alliances with key allies, and showcasing success stories that demonstrate the efficacy of your approach. By leveraging social proof, you create a ripple effect of influence that extends far beyond your own sphere of influence.

6. **Inspiring Action**: Persuasion isn't just about changing minds – it's about inspiring action and driving meaningful change. You don't just present your ideas and hope for the best; you inspire others to take action, rallying them around a shared vision and empowering them to contribute their talents and expertise to achieving your goals. By inspiring action, you transform passive

bystanders into active participants in the journey towards success.

7. **Leading by Example**: Ultimately, the most powerful form of persuasion is leading by example. You embody the values and principles you espouse, demonstrating integrity, authenticity, and unwavering commitment to your vision. Your actions speak louder than words, inspiring others to follow your lead and embrace your ideas with enthusiasm and conviction.

By mastering the art of persuasion, you'll not only achieve your goals with grace and finesse but also earn the respect and admiration of others in the process. Your ability to change minds and inspire action will serve as a shining example to others, demonstrating what it truly means to lead with wisdom, integrity, and influence. So, embrace the power of persuasion, and watch as your ideas take flight and your vision becomes reality.

Chapter 9: Navigating Sensitive Team Topics with Grace and Respect

As a badass manager, you understand that leading a team isn't just about achieving business goals – it's also about navigating the complexities of human relationships with grace and respect. In this chapter, we'll explore how to address sensitive personal topics within your team in a smart and respectful manner, fostering a culture of trust, empathy, and understanding.

1. **Create a Safe Space**: The first step in addressing sensitive topics is to create a safe and supportive environment where team members feel comfortable expressing themselves without fear of judgment or reprisal. Foster open communication, actively listen to your team members' concerns, and reassure them that their thoughts and feelings are valued and respected.

2. **Approach with Empathy**: When addressing sensitive topics, approach the conversation with empathy and

compassion. Take the time to put yourself in your team members' shoes, seeking to understand their perspective and the emotions underlying their concerns. By demonstrating empathy, you show your team members that you care about their well-being and are committed to supporting them through difficult times.

3. **Respect Privacy and Boundaries**: While it's important to foster open communication, it's equally important to respect your team members' privacy and boundaries. Avoid prying into personal matters or pressuring team members to disclose information they're not comfortable sharing. Instead, let them know that you're available to support them if and when they're ready to talk.

4. **Be Mindful of Language**: The language you use when addressing sensitive topics can have a profound impact on how your message is received. Choose your words carefully, avoiding language that is judgmental, dismissive, or insensitive. Instead, strive to communicate

with empathy, sensitivity, and respect, acknowledging the validity of your team members' feelings and experiences.

5. **Offer Support and Resources**: As a badass manager, part of your role is to support your team members through difficult times. Offer resources and support services, such as employee assistance programs or counseling services, to help team members navigate personal challenges. Let them know that they're not alone and that you're there to support them in any way you can.

6. **Lead by Example (again)**: As a leader, your actions speak louder than words. Lead by example by demonstrating vulnerability, authenticity, and a willingness to address sensitive topics openly and honestly. Show your team members that it's okay to talk about personal challenges and that seeking support is a sign of strength, not weakness.

7. **Foster a Culture of Respect and Inclusion**: Ultimately, creating an environment where sensitive topics can be addressed with grace and respect requires fostering a

culture of respect and inclusion within your team. Celebrate diversity, encourage open dialogue, and actively work to create a culture where every team member feels valued, heard, and supported.

By navigating sensitive team topics with grace and respect, you'll not only strengthen trust and cohesion within your team but also demonstrate your commitment to supporting your team members' personal well-being. Your ability to address sensitive topics with empathy and understanding will set the tone for a positive and supportive team culture where every member feels valued and respected.

Chapter 10: The Not-So-Standard Team Bonding: Tailored Fun for Your Unique Crew

As a badass manager, you understand that one size does not fit all when it comes to team bonding activities. While traditional team building exercises and networking events have their place, they may not always resonate with your unique team. In this chapter, we'll explore how to choose fun activities that are specially designed for your particular team, based on their interests, preferences, and personalities.

1. **Know Your Team**: The key to choosing the right team bonding activities is knowing your team inside and out. Take the time to get to know your team members on a personal level – their hobbies, interests, and preferences. What makes them tick? What do they enjoy doing in their free time? By understanding your team members' individual personalities and preferences, you can tailor

team bonding activities that are sure to resonate with them.

2. **Embrace Diversity**: Your team is comprised of individuals with diverse backgrounds, interests, and personalities. Embrace this diversity and choose team bonding activities that appeal to a wide range of tastes and preferences. Whether it's outdoor adventures, creative workshops, or culinary experiences, offer a variety of options to ensure that everyone feels included and engaged.

3. **Foster Collaboration**: While the primary goal of team bonding activities is to have fun and build camaraderie, they can also be an opportunity to foster collaboration and teamwork. Choose activities that encourage teamwork, problem-solving, and communication, allowing your team members to work together towards a common goal while strengthening their bonds.

4. **Get Creative**: Get Creative: Unleash your inner brainstorming ninja and concoct out-of-the-box team

bonding adventures. Think beyond the ordinary and delve into the delightfully unexpected. Whether it's a cosmic karaoke showdown or a madcap game of office mini-golf, let your imagination run wild and design experiences that'll have your team saying, "That was epic!"

5. **Incorporate Personal Touches**: Show your team members that you care by incorporating personal touches into your team bonding activities. Celebrate birthdays, milestones, and achievements with personalized gifts or special surprises. Consider including inside jokes, shared memories, or team traditions that will make the experience truly memorable and meaningful for your team.

6. **Listen to Feedback**: As a badass manager, you're always open to feedback and willing to adapt to the needs and preferences of your team. After each team bonding activity, solicit feedback from your team members to learn what worked well and what could be improved. Use this

feedback to inform future activities and ensure that each experience is better than the last.

7. **Have Fun**: Above all, remember that team bonding activities are meant to be fun and enjoyable for everyone involved. Let loose, embrace the spirit of camaraderie, and have fun alongside your team. Your enthusiasm and positive energy will set the tone for a memorable and rewarding experience that strengthens bonds and fosters a sense of belonging within your team.

By choosing fun activities that are specially designed for your unique team, you'll not only strengthen bonds and foster camaraderie but also create lasting memories and experiences that will bring your team closer together. So, get creative, embrace diversity, and tailor your team bonding activities to reflect the unique spirit of your team.

Chapter 11: The Omniscient Manager: Balancing Insight and Autonomy

As a badass manager, you possess a keen ability to stay on top of everything and know everything about everyone on your team – without resorting to micromanagement. In this chapter, we'll explore how to strike the delicate balance between being in the know and empowering your team members to thrive autonomously, all while infusing a touch of humour and seriousness where needed.

1. **The Information Connoisseur**: Like a well-seasoned detective, you possess a knack for gathering information and piecing together the puzzle of your team dynamics. From subtle cues in team meetings to casual conversations in the break room, you're constantly gathering insights into the inner workings of your team.

2. **The Art of Observation**: Rather than hovering over your team members' shoulders, you prefer to observe from a

distance, like a wise owl perched in the corner of the room. You pay attention to the little details – the furrowed brows, the hurried footsteps, the subtle changes in demeanour – and use them to inform your understanding of your team's needs and dynamics.

3. **Strategic Communication**: While you may not micromanage your team, you're a master of strategic communication. You know when to step in and offer guidance or support, and when to step back and let your team members take the reins. Your communication style is clear, concise, and purposeful, ensuring that your messages are always heard and understood.

4. **The Power of Trust**: At the heart of your management approach lies a deep trust in your team members' abilities and judgment. You empower them to take ownership of their work, knowing that they'll rise to the challenge and deliver exceptional results. Your trust is not blind – it's earned through mutual respect, open communication, and a track record of reliability.

5. **Embracing Humour**: While you take your role as manager seriously, you also know how to inject humour and levity into your interactions with your team. A well-timed joke or light-hearted quip can break the tension and foster a sense of camaraderie, making even the most mundane tasks feel like an adventure.

6. **Flexibility and Adaptability**: As a badass manager, you understand that plans are made to be flexible. You're not afraid to adapt to changing circumstances or pivot in response to new information. Your agility and adaptability enable you to stay one step ahead of the game, even when the playing field is constantly shifting.

7. **Leading by Example**: Ultimately, your ability to stay on top of everything and know everything about everyone without micromanaging stems from your exemplary leadership. You lead by example, demonstrating the same level of dedication, attention to detail, and commitment to excellence that you expect from your team. Your actions

inspire respect, trust, and admiration, making you a role model for your team members to emulate.

By striking the delicate balance between insight and autonomy, humour and seriousness, you'll not only stay on top of everything as a badass manager but also empower your team members to reach new heights of success. So, keep honing your detective skills, embracing trust and humour, and leading by example – the world is your oyster, and your team is ready to conquer it alongside you.

Chapter 12: Celebrating Diversity and Fostering Open Dialogue

As a badass manager, you recognize that a diverse team is a strong team. In this chapter, we'll explore how to support your team's diversity and promote freedom of speech and opinions while considering the company's best interests.

1. **Embracing Diversity**: Diversity isn't just a buzzword – it's a cornerstone of success in today's global marketplace. As a badass manager, you celebrate diversity in all its forms – race, gender, age, background, and perspective. You understand that diverse teams bring a wealth of ideas, experiences, and viewpoints to the table, driving innovation and creativity.

2. **Creating a Safe Space**: Foster a culture of inclusion and belonging where every team member feels valued, respected, and heard. Create a safe space where team members feel comfortable expressing their opinions,

sharing their experiences, and engaging in open dialogue without fear of judgment or reprisal.

3. **Promoting Freedom of Speech**: Encourage freedom of speech and expression within your team, recognizing that diversity of thought is essential for driving innovation and problem-solving. Respectfully challenge assumptions, encourage dissenting viewpoints, and welcome constructive criticism as opportunities for growth and learning.

4. **Setting Ground Rules**: While promoting freedom of speech, it's important to establish ground rules to ensure that discussions remain respectful and productive. Emphasize the importance of active listening, empathy, and constructive feedback. Make it clear that personal attacks, discrimination, or harassment will not be tolerated.

5. **Leading by Example**: Lead by example by actively engaging in open dialogue, soliciting input from team members, and demonstrating respect for diverse

perspectives. Show your team that you value their opinions and are committed to creating an environment where everyone feels empowered to speak up.

6. **Balancing Company Interests**: While promoting freedom of speech and diversity, it's important to strike a balance between individual expression and the company's best interests. Encourage open dialogue while ensuring that discussions remain focused on achieving the company's goals and objectives. Help your team understand how their contributions align with the company's mission and values.

7. **Resolving Conflicts**: Inevitably, conflicts may arise when diverse perspectives collide. As a badass manager, you're adept at resolving conflicts in a fair and impartial manner. Listen to all sides, seek common ground, and facilitate open communication to find mutually beneficial solutions. Use conflicts as opportunities for growth and learning, reinforcing the importance of respect, understanding, and collaboration.

By celebrating diversity, fostering open dialogue, and promoting freedom of speech and opinions while considering the company's best interests, you'll not only create a vibrant and inclusive team culture but also drive innovation, creativity, and success. So, embrace diversity, champion open communication, and lead your team to greatness with wisdom, empathy, and respect.

Chapter 13: Aligning Team Goals with Executive Vision

As a badass manager, you understand the importance of supporting senior or executive management while ensuring your team is fully aligned with the organization's strategy. In this chapter, we'll explore how to brilliantly support senior leadership, respect their decisions and interests, and effectively communicate the company's strategy to your team.

1. **Understanding Executive Vision**: Start by immersing yourself in the vision and goals set forth by senior or executive management. Gain a deep understanding of the company's strategy, priorities, and objectives. This knowledge will serve as the foundation for aligning your team's goals and initiatives with the overarching vision of the organization.

2. **Advocating for Alignment**: As a liaison between senior leadership and your team, it's your responsibility to

advocate for alignment at every turn. Clearly communicate the company's strategy to your team, emphasizing how their work contributes to the organization's overall goals. Help your team see the bigger picture and understand how their efforts fit into the broader context of the company's vision.

3. **Respecting Decisions and Interests**: While it's essential to support senior management, it's equally important to respect their decisions and interests, even if you may not always agree with them. Trust that senior leadership has the best interests of the company at heart and demonstrate your support for their decisions, even when they may be challenging or unpopular.

4. **Providing Strategic Guidance**: Act as a strategic advisor to your team, providing guidance and direction that aligns with the company's overall strategy. Help your team understand how their individual goals and projects contribute to the achievement of broader organizational

objectives. Offer insights and recommendations that support the company's long-term vision and growth.

5. **Facilitating Communication**: Facilitate open and transparent communication between senior leadership and your team. Keep your team informed about key decisions, initiatives, and updates from senior management, ensuring they feel connected to the broader organization. Encourage feedback and dialogue, creating opportunities for your team to share their thoughts and perspectives with senior leadership.

6. **Leading by Example**: Lead by example by demonstrating your commitment to the company's strategy and vision in your own actions and decisions. Show your team that you're committed to driving the organization forward. Your enthusiasm and dedication will inspire your team to follow suit, fostering a culture of alignment and unity.

7. **Celebrating Successes**: Finally, celebrate successes and milestones that align with the company's strategy, recognizing the hard work and contributions of your team

members. Highlight achievements that support the organization's goals, reinforcing the importance of alignment and collaboration in driving success. By celebrating wins together, you'll strengthen your team's connection to the company's vision and foster a sense of pride and accomplishment.

By brilliantly supporting senior or executive management, respecting their decisions and interests, and ensuring your team understands and aligns with the company's strategy, you'll create a cohesive and high-performing team that drives the organization towards its goals with confidence and determination. So, embrace your role as a strategic partner to senior leadership, and lead your team to success with vision, purpose, and unity.

Chapter 14: The Badge of Honour: Why Any Team Would Be Lucky to Have a Badass Manager

Being a badass manager isn't just a job – it's a badge of honour that any team would be proud to wear. In this chapter, we'll explore why having a badass manager is like striking gold, and why any team would consider themselves lucky to have one.

1. **The Cool Factor**: Let's face it – having a badass manager instantly ups your team's cool factor. With their sharp wit, unwavering confidence, and knack for getting things done, badass managers bring a certain swagger to the table that's hard to ignore. Who wouldn't want to be part of a team led by someone who exudes charisma and charm?

2. **The Ultimate Support System**: Badass managers aren't just leaders – they're mentors, coaches, and cheerleaders rolled into one. They're there to support their team members through thick and thin, offering guidance,

encouragement, and a shoulder to lean on when needed. With a badass manager in your corner, you know you've got someone who's always got your back.

3. **The Mastermind of Success**: Behind every successful team is a badass manager pulling the strings and orchestrating the magic. With their strategic vision, impeccable leadership skills, and knack for bringing out the best in their team, badass managers are the secret sauce that turns good teams into great ones. They know how to inspire greatness, drive results, and lead their team to victory time and time again.

4. **The Fun Factor**: Badass managers know that work doesn't have to be all serious business – it can also be a whole lot of fun. With their quick wit, playful humour, and knack for keeping things light and entertaining, badass managers know how to inject a healthy dose of fun into the workplace. Whether it's a witty one-liner, a hilarious team outing, or a silly inside joke, they know how to keep morale high and spirits lifted.

5. **The Fearless Leader**: Badass managers aren't afraid to take risks, make tough decisions, and blaze their own trail. They're fearless leaders who aren't afraid to challenge the status quo, push boundaries, and lead by example. With their unwavering confidence and unshakeable resolve, they inspire their team to take risks, think outside the box, and reach for the stars.

6. **The Champion of Diversity**: Badass managers embrace diversity in all its forms and champion inclusivity and equality in the workplace. They recognize the value of diverse perspectives and experiences and work tirelessly to create a culture where everyone feels valued, respected, and empowered to succeed. With a badass manager at the helm, you know you're part of a team that celebrates diversity and fosters a sense of belonging for all.

7. **The Heart and Soul**: At the end of the day, what truly sets a badass manager apart is their heart and soul. They're not just leaders – they're compassionate, empathetic, and deeply invested in the success and well-being of their

team members. They lead with integrity, authenticity, and a genuine desire to see their team succeed. With a badass manager leading the way, you know you're part of a team that's destined for greatness.

So, if you're lucky enough to have a badass manager leading your team, consider yourself truly fortunate. With their wit, wisdom, and unwavering support, they're the secret sauce that makes any team shine. So, wear your badge of honour proudly, and know that you're part of something truly special.

Chapter 15: From Bad to Badass: Turning a Rough Day into a Day of Triumph

Even the most badass managers encounter rough days, but what sets them apart is their ability to turn adversity into opportunity. In this chapter, we'll explore how a badass manager can transform a bad day into a day full of growth, resilience, and ultimately, triumph.

1. **Embracing Resilience**: The mark of a true badass manager is their resilience in the face of adversity. Instead of letting setbacks derail them, they embrace challenges as opportunities for growth and learning. They understand that setbacks are a natural part of the journey and use them as fuel to propel themselves and their team forward.

2. **Finding the Silver Lining**: Bad days are full of silver linings – you just have to know where to look. A badass manager has a knack for finding the positive amidst the negative, reframing setbacks as opportunities for growth

and innovation. They see challenges as a chance to stretch their creativity, test their limits, and emerge stronger on the other side.

3. **Leading by Example**: In times of adversity, a badass manager leads by example, demonstrating resilience, optimism, and determination in the face of adversity. They show their team that setbacks are temporary roadblocks, not insurmountable obstacles, and inspire them to persevere with unwavering confidence and resolve.

4. **Seizing Opportunities**: A badass manager knows that every setback is an opportunity in disguise. Instead of dwelling on what went wrong, they focus on what they can do to make things right. They seize opportunities to learn from their mistakes, course-correct their approach, and emerge stronger and more resilient than before.

5. **Cultivating a Positive Mindset**: A positive mindset is the secret weapon of a badass manager. They approach challenges with optimism, confidence, and a can-do

attitude, knowing that their mindset has the power to shape their reality. They refuse to be bogged down by negativity and instead choose to focus on the possibilities and opportunities that lie ahead.

6. **Practising Self-Care**: In the midst of a bad day, a badass manager knows the importance of taking care of themselves. They prioritize self-care, whether it's taking a walk outside, practising mindfulness, or indulging in a favourite hobby. By replenishing their own energy and resilience, they're better equipped to lead their team through challenging times.

7. **Celebrating Small Victories**: Even on the toughest of days, there are always small victories to celebrate. A badass manager takes the time to acknowledge and celebrate these wins, no matter how small, recognizing that they're a testament to their team's resilience, determination, and perseverance.

By turning a bad day into a day of triumph, a badass manager demonstrates their resilience, optimism, and unwavering commitment to their team's success. They show that with the right mindset, anything is possible, and that even in the face of adversity, there are always opportunities for growth, learning, and ultimately, triumph. So, embrace the challenges, seize the opportunities, and let your badassery shine through, turning every bad day into a day of triumph.

Chapter 16: Unleashing the Badassery: Key Traits for Navigating Challenging Circumstances

In the high-stakes world of management, a badass manager possesses a unique set of traits that allow them to thrive amidst even the most challenging circumstances. In this chapter, we'll explore the key traits that enable a badass manager to turn every situation into gold.

1. **Adaptability**: A badass manager is like a chameleon, able to adapt seamlessly to changing circumstances and environments. They thrive in uncertainty, embracing change as an opportunity for growth and innovation. Whether faced with a sudden crisis or shifting market trends, they pivot with ease, turning obstacles into opportunities and emerging stronger on the other side.

2. **Resilience**: Resilience is the backbone of a badass manager's success. They have an unshakeable belief in their ability to overcome adversity, bouncing back from setbacks with renewed determination and resolve. Instead of letting failure derail them, they use it as fuel to propel themselves forward, turning setbacks into stepping stones on the path to success.

3. **Emotional Intelligence**: A badass manager possesses keen emotional intelligence, able to navigate complex interpersonal dynamics with grace and finesse. They understand the power of empathy, actively listening to their team members' concerns and perspectives, and forging strong relationships built on trust and mutual respect. By fostering a culture of psychological safety, they create an environment where team members feel empowered to speak up, take risks, and innovate.

4. **Strategic Vision**: At the heart of every badass manager is a strategic vision that guides their decisions and actions. They have a clear understanding of their organization's

goals, objectives, and priorities, and use this knowledge to inform their strategic approach. Whether devising a new business strategy or navigating a crisis, they keep their eye on the big picture, always thinking several steps ahead.

5. **Creativity**: A badass manager is a master of creativity, able to think outside the box and find innovative solutions to complex problems. They're not afraid to challenge the status quo, break rules, or take calculated risks in pursuit of their goals. With their boundless imagination and entrepreneurial spirit, they turn constraints into opportunities, transforming challenges into triumphs.

6. **Decisiveness**: In times of uncertainty, a badass manager doesn't hesitate to make tough decisions. They trust their instincts, weigh the pros and cons, and act decisively, even in the face of ambiguity. By maintaining a cool head and exercising sound judgment, they inspire confidence and trust in their team, rallying them to action and driving results.

7. **Integrity**: Integrity is the cornerstone of a badass manager's leadership style. They lead with honesty, transparency, and integrity, earning the trust and respect of their team members through their actions and words. They're true to their values and principles, never compromising their integrity for short-term gain. By leading with integrity, they set the standard for ethical behaviour and create a culture of accountability and trust.

By embodying these key traits, a badass manager navigates challenging circumstances with poise, confidence, and grace. They turn every situation into an opportunity for growth, innovation, and success, transforming adversity into triumph and paving the way for their team's greatness. So, embrace your inner badassery, and let your key traits shine through as you navigate the complexities of leadership with wisdom, courage, and resilience.

Chapter 17: Leading Through Disagreement: Executing Difficult Tasks with Conviction and Collaboration

As a badass manager, there are moments when you're tasked with executing difficult tasks that may not align with your personal beliefs or preferences. However, your ability to lead through disagreement is a testament to your resilience, adaptability, and commitment to your team's success. In this chapter, we'll explore how a badass manager executes challenging tasks with conviction and collaboration, while also convincing and encouraging the team of their importance.

1. **Understanding the Big Picture**: Before diving into executing a difficult task, a badass manager takes the time to understand the big picture. They consider the broader organizational goals, strategic priorities, and potential implications of the task at hand. By gaining clarity on the why behind the task, they're better equipped to communicate its importance to the team.

2. **Communicating with Transparency**: Transparency is key when executing difficult tasks. A badass manager communicates openly and honestly with the team, explaining the rationale behind the task and addressing any concerns or questions that may arise. They're transparent about their own reservations or disagreements, but also emphasize the importance of supporting the team and the organization as a whole.

3. **Leading by Example**: A badass manager leads by example, demonstrating their commitment to executing difficult tasks with grace and professionalism. They roll up their sleeves and dive into the work alongside their team, showing that they're willing to do whatever it takes to get the job done. By leading from the front, they inspire confidence and motivate the team to follow their lead.

4. **Finding Common Ground**: In moments of disagreement, a badass manager seeks to find common ground with the team. They encourage open dialogue and constructive feedback, allowing team members to voice their concerns

and perspectives. By actively listening and engaging in dialogue, they foster a sense of collaboration and ownership, ensuring that everyone feels heard and valued.

5. **Highlighting the Benefits**: While executing difficult tasks may be challenging, a badass manager highlights the potential benefits and opportunities that come with them. They paint a clear picture of the positive outcomes that can be achieved by completing the task successfully, motivating the team to stay focused and committed despite any initial reservations.

6. **Providing Support and Resources**: A badass manager provides the necessary support and resources to help the team execute difficult tasks effectively. Whether it's offering additional training, providing access to tools and resources, or assigning dedicated support staff, they ensure that the team has everything they need to succeed. By removing barriers and obstacles, they empower the

team to tackle the task with confidence and determination.

7. **Celebrating Achievements**: Finally, a badass manager celebrates achievements and milestones along the way, recognizing the hard work and dedication of the team. They acknowledge the team's efforts in executing the difficult task, highlighting the progress made and the impact of their contributions. By celebrating successes, they reinforce the importance of collaboration, resilience, and teamwork in overcoming challenges and achieving success.

By executing difficult tasks with conviction and collaboration, a badass manager demonstrates their commitment to their team's success and the organization's goals. They lead with transparency, integrity, and empathy, inspiring confidence and trust in their leadership. So, embrace the challenge, rally the team, and lead with conviction as you navigate through difficult tasks with grace and determination.

Chapter 18: Dispelling Myths: What a Badass Manager Isn't

In the realm of management lore, myths abound regarding the enigmatic badass manager. Let's debunk these misconceptions and shed light on what a badass manager is not, with a touch of clever wit.

1. **A Dictator in Disguise**: Contrary to popular belief, a badass manager is not a tyrant ruling with an iron fist. They eschew authoritarianism in favour of collaborative leadership, understanding that true strength lies in empowering others rather than asserting dominance.

2. **The Office Oracle**: While possessing remarkable insight, a badass manager is not clairvoyant. They don't have a crystal ball to predict every twist and turn in the corporate landscape. Instead, they rely on strategic thinking, adaptability, and a healthy dose of intuition to navigate uncertainty.

3. **A Miracle Worker**: Despite their superhero vibes, a badass manager is not endowed with magical powers. They can't wave a wand and instantly solve all problems. Instead, they rely on hard work, creativity, and resourcefulness to overcome challenges and drive success.

4. **A Lone Wolf**: Far from being a solitary figure, a badass manager is not a lone wolf roaming the corporate wilderness. They understand the value of teamwork and collaboration, fostering a culture of inclusivity and cooperation where every team member plays a vital role.

5. **A Yes-Man (or Woman)**: A badass manager is not a puppet blindly nodding in agreement with every decision. They are independent thinkers who aren't afraid to challenge the status quo, offer dissenting opinions, and advocate for what they believe is right, even if it means rocking the boat.

6. **The Office Clown**: While possessing a keen sense of humour, a badass manager is not a mere jester entertaining the masses. They use humour strategically to

foster camaraderie, diffuse tension, and create a positive work environment, all while maintaining professionalism and respect.

7. **A Know-It-All**: Despite their intellectual prowess, a badass manager is not omniscient. They recognize the value of lifelong learning and remain humble in the face of their own limitations. They seek input from others, welcome diverse perspectives, and continuously strive to expand their knowledge and skills.

In summary, a badass manager is not defined by stereotypes or misconceptions but by their unique blend of leadership qualities, authenticity, and resilience. They defy expectations, challenge norms, and inspire greatness in themselves and others. So, let's dispel the myths and embrace the true essence of what it means to be a badass manager.

Chapter 19: The Badass Manager vs. Michael Scott: Similarities and Differences

In the annals of fictional management, one character stands out as both beloved and cringe-inducing: Michael Scott from the American series "The Office." Let's explore the similarities and differences between the iconic regional manager and the archetype of a badass manager.

Similarities:

1. **Charismatic Leadership**: Like Michael Scott, a badass manager possesses an undeniable charisma that captivates their team. They both have a knack for winning over hearts and minds with their charm, humour, and larger-than-life personality.

2. **Unconventional Approach**: Both Michael Scott and a badass manager are known for their unconventional

approach to leadership. They're not afraid to think outside the box, take risks, and break the rules in pursuit of their goals.

3. **Genuine Care**: Despite their quirks, both Michael Scott and a badass manager genuinely care about their team members. They may have unconventional ways of showing it, but at the core, their intentions are rooted in a desire to support and uplift their team.

Differences:

1. **Strategic Thinking**: While Michael Scott tends to operate on impulse and emotion, a badass manager approaches leadership with strategic thinking and foresight. They make decisions based on careful analysis and consideration of long-term implications, rather than spur-of-the-moment whims.

2. **Emotional Intelligence**: A badass manager possesses a high level of emotional intelligence, allowing them to navigate complex interpersonal dynamics with finesse. In contrast, Michael Scott often struggles with social cues

and lacks self-awareness, leading to awkward and cringe-worthy moments.

3. **Professionalism**: While Michael Scott's antics often blur the lines of professionalism, a badass manager maintains a level of professionalism and integrity in all aspects of their leadership. They know when to be serious and when to inject humour, striking a balance that fosters a positive work environment.

4. **Empowerment vs. Micromanagement**: A badass manager empowers their team members to take ownership of their work and make decisions autonomously. In contrast, Michael Scott tends to micromanage and insert himself into every aspect of his team's work, often stifling creativity and innovation.

5. **Growth Mindset**: A badass manager embraces a growth mindset, continuously seeking opportunities for learning, growth, and improvement. They encourage their team members to do the same, fostering a culture of innovation and development. Michael Scott, on the other hand, often

resists change and fails to embrace opportunities for personal and professional growth.

In summary, while Michael Scott and a badass manager share certain charismatic qualities, they differ significantly in their approach to leadership, emotional intelligence, professionalism, empowerment, and growth mindset. While Michael Scott may be entertaining to watch on screen, a badass manager embodies the essence of effective and inspiring leadership in the real world.

Chapter 20: The Joy of Having a Badass Manager

Having a badass manager at the helm isn't just a stroke of luck – it's a game-changer that can transform the entire workplace experience. Let's delve into the myriad reasons why being on a team with a badass manager as your boss feels absolutely fantastic.

1. **Inspired Confidence**: Under the guidance of a badass manager, team members feel a surge of inspired confidence coursing through their veins. They know they have a leader who believes in their abilities, champions their success, and empowers them to reach new heights.

2. **Valued Contribution**: A badass manager doesn't just see team members as cogs in the machine – they value each individual's unique contributions and perspectives. Team members feel seen, heard, and appreciated for their skills,

ideas, and efforts, fostering a sense of belonging and significance within the team.

3. **Clear Direction**: With a badass manager at the helm, team members have a clear sense of direction and purpose. They know exactly what's expected of them, where they're headed, and how their work contributes to the larger goals of the team and organization. This clarity instills a sense of focus and motivation that fuels their productivity and drive.

4. **Supportive Environment**: Team members thrive in the supportive environment cultivated by a badass manager. They feel comfortable speaking up, sharing their thoughts and concerns, and seeking guidance when needed. With a leader who has their back, they're emboldened to take risks, make mistakes, and learn and grow from their experiences.

5. **Growth Opportunities**: A badass manager is committed to the growth and development of their team members. They provide ample opportunities for learning, skill-

building, and professional advancement, helping team members unlock their full potential and pursue their career aspirations with confidence and enthusiasm.

6. **Celebrated Wins**: In a team led by a badass manager, victories – big and small – are celebrated with gusto. Team members bask in the glow of their accomplishments, knowing that their hard work and achievements are recognized and valued by their leader. This culture of celebration fosters a sense of pride, camaraderie, and shared success within the team.

7. **Fun and Fulfilment**: Above all, being on a team with a badass manager as your boss is just plain fun. Team members enjoy coming to work each day, knowing that they'll be greeted with positivity, humour, and a spirit of camaraderie. With a leader who knows how to balance hard work with a healthy dose of laughter and levity, every day feels like an adventure filled with excitement and fulfilment.

In conclusion, having a badass manager as your boss isn't just a professional blessing – it's a source of joy, inspiration, and fulfilment that transforms the workplace experience in the best possible way. With a leader who believes in their team, values their contributions, and fosters a culture of support and growth, team members feel empowered to achieve greatness and truly thrive in their roles.

Chapter 21: The Unsung Hero: How Recognition Finds the Badass Manager

In the realm of leadership, the badass manager stands out not for seeking recognition or accolades, but for their unwavering dedication, integrity, and commitment to their team. Despite their humble approach, recognition and awards have a way of finding them, driven by the undeniable impact of their leadership. Let's explore how the badass manager becomes an unsung hero, celebrated for their remarkable contributions.

1. **Leading by Example**: The badass manager leads not for glory, but because it's simply who they are. They exemplify the qualities of effective leadership every day, inspiring their team with their work ethic, integrity, and passion for excellence. Their actions speak louder than words, earning them the respect and admiration of their peers and superiors alike.

2. **Putting the Team First**: Unlike leaders who seek the spotlight, the badass manager prioritizes the success and well-being of their team above all else. They shine a spotlight on their team members' achievements, empowering them to shine and basking in their collective success. By putting the team first, they create a culture of collaboration, trust, and camaraderie that breeds success.

3. **Making a Lasting Impact**: The badass manager isn't motivated by short-term gains or fleeting recognition – they're driven by the desire to make a lasting impact. They invest in the growth and development of their team members, mentoring, coaching, and empowering them to reach their full potential. Their legacy is measured not in awards or accolades, but in the lives they've touched and the positive change they've inspired.

4. **Humble Confidence**: Despite their undeniable achievements, the badass manager remains humble and grounded, never seeking the spotlight or boasting about their accomplishments. They understand that true

leadership is about service, not self-promotion, and they prefer to let their actions speak for themselves. Their quiet confidence and humility only serve to endear them further to those around them.

5. **Respected by Peers**: In the eyes of their peers, the badass manager is a beacon of integrity, professionalism, and excellence. They command respect not through flashy titles or grand gestures, but through their consistent demonstration of leadership qualities that inspire trust and admiration. Their reputation precedes them, earning them the admiration and respect of colleagues across the organization.

6. **Impactful Results**: Ultimately, the badass manager's greatest recognition comes in the form of tangible results and achievements. Whether it's surpassing performance targets, driving innovation, or fostering a culture of excellence, their impact is felt far and wide throughout the organization. Their track record of success speaks for

itself, earning them the recognition and admiration of leaders at all levels.

In conclusion, while the badass manager may not seek recognition or awards, their remarkable leadership inevitably attracts attention and acclaim. Driven by a deep-seated commitment to their team and a passion for excellence, they become unsung heroes whose impact transcends titles and accolades. Their legacy is measured not in plaques or trophies, but in the lives they've touched and the positive change they've inspired.

Chapter 22: Rebels with a Cause: How the Badass Manager Earns Respect through Rebellion

In the world of management, conformity is often valued over rebellion, but the badass manager knows when to bend the rules for the greater good. With a keen sense of purpose and a healthy dose of courage, they navigate the fine line between rebellion and responsibility, earning respect for their actions along the way. Let's explore how the badass manager gets away with being occasionally rebellious for a good cause while still commanding respect from their team and peers.

1. **Fighting for What's Right**: The badass manager isn't afraid to challenge the status quo and push back against unjust or outdated policies and practices. When they see something that's not working or doesn't align with their values, they speak up and take action, even if it means rocking the boat. Their rebellious spirit is fuelled by a

deep-seated commitment to doing what's right, and their team respects them for their integrity and courage.

2. **Championing Innovation**: Rebellion isn't always about breaking rules – sometimes, it's about pushing boundaries and thinking outside the box. The badass manager embraces a culture of innovation and experimentation, encouraging their team to explore new ideas and approaches. They're not afraid to challenge conventional wisdom and take calculated risks in pursuit of game-changing innovations that drive the organization forward.

3. **Leading by Example**: The badass manager leads by example, demonstrating their rebellious spirit through their actions rather than just their words. They're willing to roll up their sleeves and get their hands dirty, leading from the front and showing their team that they're not afraid to take risks or challenge the status quo. Their authenticity and fearlessness inspire respect and admiration from their team members, who see them as a true leader worth following.

4. **Earning Trust through Transparency**: While rebellion can be risky, the badass manager earns trust and respect through transparency and honesty. They communicate openly with their team about their motivations and intentions, explaining the reasoning behind their actions and inviting feedback and collaboration. By fostering a culture of trust and transparency, they build strong relationships with their team members, who respect them for their integrity and authenticity.

5. **Delivering Results**: Ultimately, the badass manager's rebellious actions are justified by the results they deliver. Whether it's challenging the status quo, championing innovation, or fighting for what's right, their actions lead to positive outcomes that benefit the organization as a whole. Their track record of success speaks for itself, earning them the respect and admiration of their team and peers.

In conclusion, the badass manager knows that rebellion isn't about breaking rules for the sake of it – it's about challenging the status quo and pushing boundaries for the greater good. By fighting for what's right, championing innovation, leading by example, earning trust through transparency, and delivering results, they earn respect for their rebellious actions while still upholding their integrity and professionalism. They're rebels with a cause, and their team respects them all the more for it.

Chapter 23: Silent Champions: How the Badass Manager Supports Others Without Them Even Knowing

In the world of leadership, there are those who seek the spotlight and those who work tirelessly behind the scenes to support others. The badass manager falls into the latter category, quietly championing their team members and co-workers without fanfare or recognition. Let's explore how the badass manager supports others without them even knowing, promoting the success of their team members and co-workers in subtle yet impactful ways.

1. **Providing Opportunities**: The badass manager is a master at creating opportunities for their team members and co-workers to shine. They're constantly on the lookout for ways to elevate others, whether it's by assigning them challenging projects, recommending them for new opportunities, or connecting them with influential

contacts. By providing these opportunities behind the scenes, they empower others to reach their full potential and achieve their career goals.

2. **Offering Guidance and Mentorship**: Behind closed doors, the badass manager serves as a trusted advisor and mentor to their team members and co-workers. They offer guidance, share insights, and provide constructive feedback to help others grow and develop in their roles. Whether it's a casual conversation over coffee or a formal mentoring session, they're always there to support and encourage others on their professional journey.

3. **Advocating for Recognition**: The badass manager is a fierce advocate for their team members and co-workers, tirelessly championing their accomplishments and advocating for recognition on their behalf. They're not afraid to sing their praises to senior leadership, highlight their achievements in team meetings, or nominate them for awards and accolades. By shining a spotlight on their

successes, they ensure that others receive the recognition they deserve for their hard work and contributions.

4. **Creating a Culture of Support**: In the day-to-day interactions of the workplace, the badass manager fosters a culture of support and collaboration where everyone feels valued and appreciated. They're quick to offer a helping hand, lend an ear, or provide encouragement to those in need. Whether it's offering a word of encouragement during a tough day or celebrating a colleague's success, they're always there to lift others up and promote a sense of camaraderie and teamwork.

5. **Leading by Example**: Perhaps most importantly, the badass manager leads by example, embodying the values of humility, generosity, and selflessness in their own actions. They don't seek recognition or praise for themselves – instead, they focus on lifting others up and promoting their success. By leading with integrity and compassion, they inspire others to do the same, creating a

ripple effect of support and kindness throughout the organization.

In conclusion, the badass manager is a silent champion who supports others without them even knowing, promoting the success of their team members and co-workers in subtle yet impactful ways. Through providing opportunities, offering guidance and mentorship, advocating for recognition, creating a culture of support, and leading by example, they empower others to reach their full potential and thrive in their roles. They may not seek the spotlight, but their impact is felt far and wide, leaving a lasting legacy of support, encouragement, and empowerment in their wake.

Chapter 24: Embracing Unpopularity: Why the Badass Manager Isn't Always Liked by Others

In the dynamic landscape of leadership, the badass manager stands out as a beacon of strength, integrity, and authenticity. Yet, despite their best intentions, they may find themselves at odds with certain individuals who aspire to emulate their badassery but fall short. Let's explore why the badass manager isn't always liked by others – not because of their own shortcomings, but because of the expectations and insecurities of those who seek to emulate them.

1. **Setting High Standards**: The badass manager sets the bar high for themselves and their team, expecting nothing less than excellence in everything they do. While this commitment to excellence inspires respect and admiration from some, others may feel intimidated or threatened by the high standards they set. Those who struggle to meet

these standards may resent the badass manager for holding them accountable and pushing them out of their comfort zone.

2. **Challenging the Status Quo**: True to their rebellious nature, the badass manager isn't afraid to challenge the status quo and push back against outdated or ineffective practices. While this willingness to question authority and innovate may earn them praise from forward-thinking individuals, it can also ruffle the feathers of those who are resistant to change or comfortable with the status quo. Those who cling to tradition may view the badass manager's actions as disruptive or confrontational, leading to friction and animosity.

3. **Embracing Unpopular Decisions**: In their quest to do what's right for the team and the organization, the badass manager isn't afraid to make tough decisions – even if they're unpopular. Whether it's restructuring the team, reallocating resources, or holding individuals accountable for their performance, they prioritize the long-term

success of the organization over short-term popularity. While some may appreciate their decisiveness and clarity of vision, others may resent them for making difficult choices that challenge their comfort or disrupt the status quo.

4. **Exuding Confidence and Authenticity**: The badass manager exudes an air of confidence, authenticity, and self-assuredness that commands respect and admiration from those around them. Yet, for individuals who struggle with their own insecurities or lack confidence in their abilities, this unwavering confidence may be perceived as arrogance or aloofness. Those who feel threatened by the badass manager's self-assurance may project their own insecurities onto them, leading to misunderstandings and friction in their interactions.

5. **Inspiring Jealousy and Envy**: At the end of the day, the badass manager's undeniable charisma, success, and impact may inspire feelings of jealousy and envy in those who aspire to emulate them but fall short. Rather than

acknowledging their own shortcomings and working to improve themselves, these individuals may resent the badass manager for their success and seek to undermine or discredit them in an attempt to elevate themselves.

In conclusion, the badass manager isn't always liked by others – not because of any fault or failing on their part, but because of the expectations and insecurities of those who seek to emulate them but fall short. By setting high standards, challenging the status quo, embracing unpopular decisions, exuding confidence and authenticity, and inspiring jealousy and envy, the badass manager may find themselves at odds with certain individuals who are unable to rise to the challenge. Yet, despite the friction and animosity they may encounter, the badass manager remains steadfast in their commitment to leading with integrity, authenticity, and courage, knowing that their actions are driven by a desire to do what's right for their team and the organization as a whole.

Chapter 25: Transformative Leadership: How the Badass Manager Turns Critics into Grateful Allies

In the dynamic landscape of leadership, the badass manager possesses a unique ability to transform sceptics and critics into grateful allies through their unwavering commitment to growth, development, and authenticity. Let's explore how the badass manager helps people who initially don't like them to become better versions of themselves, ultimately leading to gratitude and appreciation for their impact.

1. **Leading by Example**: The badass manager leads by example, embodying the qualities of integrity, authenticity, and compassion in their own actions. Despite initial reservations or scepticism from others, they remain steadfast in their commitment to doing what's right, setting a positive example for those around them to follow. By demonstrating their commitment to growth

and improvement, they inspire others to do the same, leading to positive transformation over time.

2. **Providing Support and Guidance**: Behind the scenes, the badass manager provides support and guidance to individuals who may initially resist or resent their leadership. They offer a listening ear, share valuable insights, and provide constructive feedback to help others overcome their challenges and reach their full potential. Rather than dismissing or ignoring dissenting voices, they actively seek to understand their concerns and address them with empathy and understanding.

3. **Offering Opportunities for Growth**: The badass manager creates opportunities for growth and development, even for those who may initially doubt or question their leadership. They challenge individuals to step outside their comfort zones, take on new challenges, and push themselves to new heights of excellence. By providing opportunities for growth and advancement, they

empower others to unlock their full potential and achieve success beyond their wildest dreams.

4. **Fostering a Culture of Collaboration**: In the team environment cultivated by the badass manager, collaboration and teamwork are paramount. They encourage open communication, mutual respect, and shared accountability, creating a culture where everyone feels valued and supported. Through collaboration, individuals who initially clashed with the badass manager find common ground and discover the power of working together towards a shared vision.

5. **Celebrating Successes**: As individuals grow and develop under the badass manager's leadership, their successes are celebrated and acknowledged with genuine enthusiasm and appreciation. The badass manager recognizes the contributions of all team members, regardless of their initial reservations or doubts, and celebrates their achievements with pride and gratitude. By acknowledging their growth and progress, they reinforce

the importance of continuous improvement and foster a culture of gratitude and appreciation.

In conclusion, the badass manager has a remarkable ability to turn critics into grateful allies through their transformative leadership approach. By leading by example, providing support and guidance, offering opportunities for growth, fostering a culture of collaboration, and celebrating successes, they empower individuals to overcome their initial scepticism and resistance and become better versions of themselves. In the end, those who once doubted or disliked the badass manager find themselves grateful for the positive impact they've had on their personal and professional growth journey.

Chapter 26: Actions Speak Louder: How the Badass Manager Guides Talkers to Walkers

In the realm of leadership, the badass manager values action over mere words and refuses to tolerate empty promises or hollow rhetoric. When faced with individuals who talk a big game but fail to deliver results, they see an opportunity for growth and transformation. Let's explore how the badass manager helps these talkers become walkers, guiding them towards tangible actions and meaningful progress.

1. **Setting Clear Expectations**: The badass manager begins by setting clear expectations and standards for performance, emphasizing the importance of action and results over empty talk. They communicate their expectations openly and transparently, leaving no room for ambiguity or misunderstanding. By establishing a culture of accountability and performance, they create a

framework for individuals to channel their talk into meaningful action.

2. **Holding Individuals Accountable**: When individuals fail to follow through on their commitments or deliver on their promises, the badass manager holds them accountable in a firm yet fair manner. They address issues directly and constructively, providing feedback and guidance to help individuals understand the impact of their actions – or lack thereof. By holding individuals accountable for their performance, they create a sense of urgency and accountability that motivates them to take action and deliver results.

3. **Providing Support and Resources**: Recognizing that talkers may lack the skills, knowledge, or resources to translate their words into action, the badass manager provides the support and resources they need to succeed. Whether it's additional training, mentoring, or access to tools and resources, they ensure that individuals have everything they need to overcome obstacles and achieve

their goals. By providing support and guidance, they empower individuals to take ownership of their development and make meaningful progress.

4. **Leading by Example**: The badass manager leads by example, demonstrating their commitment to action and results in their own actions and behaviours. They walk the walk, rather than just talking the talk, and inspire others to do the same through their actions. By modelling the behaviour they expect from others, they create a culture of accountability and performance that motivates individuals to step up and deliver their best.

5. **Celebrating Progress**: As individuals make progress towards their goals and begin to translate their talk into action, the badass manager celebrates their achievements with genuine enthusiasm and appreciation. They recognize the effort and dedication required to turn talk into action, and celebrate each milestone and success along the way. By celebrating progress, they reinforce the

importance of action and encourage individuals to continue striving for excellence.

In conclusion, the badass manager refuses to tolerate empty talk or hollow promises and instead guides talkers to become walkers through their transformative leadership approach. By setting clear expectations, holding individuals accountable, providing support and resources, leading by example, and celebrating progress, they empower individuals to translate their words into meaningful action and achieve tangible results. In doing so, they create a culture of accountability, performance, and excellence that drives success for the individual and the team as a whole.

Chapter 27: The Illusion of Arrogance: Understanding the Badass Manager's True Nature

In the complex landscape of leadership, the badass manager may sometimes be perceived as arrogant due to their unwavering confidence, assertiveness, and strong sense of self-assurance. However, beneath this facade lies a deeper truth – the badass manager is anything but arrogant. Let's explore how the badass manager's apparent arrogance is merely a surface-level illusion, masking their true nature of humility, authenticity, and compassion.

1. **Confidence, Not Arrogance**: The badass manager exudes an air of confidence that may be mistaken for arrogance by those who don't know them well. However, this confidence stems not from a place of superiority or entitlement, but from a deep-rooted belief in their abilities and a track record of success. They trust in their

judgment, skills, and expertise, and aren't afraid to assert themselves when necessary – but their confidence is tempered by humility and self-awareness.

2. **Assertiveness, Not Domination**: In their interactions with others, the badass manager may come across as assertive and decisive, leading some to perceive them as arrogant or domineering. However, their assertiveness is driven not by a desire to dominate or control others, but by a commitment to achieving results and driving progress. They're not afraid to speak up, voice their opinions, and take charge when needed, but they do so with respect and consideration for others' perspectives.

3. **Strong Leadership, Not Ego**: The badass manager's strong leadership style may be misconstrued as ego-driven behaviour, but in reality, their actions are guided by a genuine desire to lead and inspire others. They prioritize the success and well-being of their team above their own ego, and aren't afraid to make tough decisions or take bold risks in pursuit of their goals. Their

leadership is rooted in humility, empathy, and a deep sense of responsibility to those they lead.

4. **Authenticity, Not Pretence**: Despite their confident exterior, the badass manager remains true to themselves and their values, refusing to compromise their authenticity for the sake of appearances. They're not interested in putting on airs or pretending to be something they're not – what you see is what you get with them. Their authenticity shines through in everything they do, from their words and actions to their relationships with others.

5. **Compassion, Not Indifference**: Beneath their tough exterior lies a heart of compassion and empathy for others. While the badass manager may come across as tough and uncompromising at times, they genuinely care about the well-being and success of their team members and colleagues. They're always there to offer support, guidance, and encouragement when needed, and go out

of their way to ensure that others feel valued and appreciated.

In conclusion, while the badass manager may sometimes be perceived as arrogant due to their confidence, assertiveness, and strong leadership style, this perception belies their true nature of humility, authenticity, and compassion. They're not driven by ego or a desire for power and control, but by a genuine commitment to leading and inspiring others towards success. By understanding the difference between arrogance and confidence, we can appreciate the unique qualities that make the badass manager an effective and inspiring leader.

Chapter 28: Provocative Leadership: How the Badass Manager Sparks Innovation Through Controversial Statements

In the realm of leadership, the badass manager isn't afraid to shake things up and challenge the status quo by putting forward provocative statements – even if they personally disagree with them. By doing so, they ignite lively brainstorming sessions and discussions that stimulate creativity, foster critical thinking, and drive innovation. Let's delve into how the badass manager leverages controversial statements to spark productive dialogue and unlock new perspectives.

1. **Stimulating Critical Thinking**: When the badass manager puts forward a controversial statement, they're not seeking agreement or validation – they're seeking to stimulate critical thinking and encourage individuals to question assumptions and explore new ideas. By challenging conventional wisdom and pushing

boundaries, they compel their team members to think outside the box and consider alternative perspectives that they may not have otherwise considered.

2. **Encouraging Diverse Perspectives**: Controversial statements have a way of eliciting diverse perspectives and opinions from individuals with different backgrounds, experiences, and viewpoints. The badass manager welcomes this diversity of thought and encourages open dialogue and debate, creating a safe space for individuals to express their opinions and contribute to the conversation. By embracing diverse perspectives, they foster a culture of inclusivity and creativity that fuels innovation and breakthrough thinking.

3. **Fostering Innovation**: Controversial statements often serve as catalysts for innovation, inspiring individuals to challenge assumptions, explore new possibilities, and think creatively about how to solve complex problems. The badass manager recognizes the power of provocative

thinking to drive innovation and breakthroughs, and actively encourages their team members to push the boundaries of what's possible. By fostering a culture of experimentation and risk-taking, they empower individuals to unleash their full creative potential and drive meaningful change.

4. **Strengthening Team Dynamics**: While controversial statements may initially spark heated debate and disagreement, they ultimately strengthen team dynamics by fostering collaboration, trust, and mutual respect. Through open dialogue and respectful discourse, individuals learn to listen to and understand different perspectives, leading to greater empathy and cooperation. The badass manager plays a pivotal role in facilitating these discussions and ensuring that they remain constructive and productive, even in the face of disagreement.

5. **Driving Action and Results**: Ultimately, the goal of putting forward controversial statements isn't just to

spark discussion for its own sake – it's to drive action and results. The badass manager leverages provocative thinking to challenge the status quo, identify opportunities for improvement, and drive meaningful change within the organization. By inspiring individuals to think differently and embrace new ideas, they empower their team to innovate, collaborate, and achieve breakthrough results.

In conclusion, the badass manager isn't afraid to put forward controversial statements to ignite good brainstorming and discussion. By stimulating critical thinking, encouraging diverse perspectives, fostering innovation, strengthening team dynamics, and driving action and results, they leverage provocative thinking as a powerful tool for driving positive change and unlocking new opportunities for growth and success. Through their bold leadership approach, they inspire their team to think differently, challenge assumptions, and embrace innovation in pursuit of their collective goals.

Chapter 29: The Enigma of the Badass Manager: Embracing Mystery in Leadership

In the dynamic world of leadership, the badass manager often possesses an aura of enigma and mystery that sets them apart from their peers. While their actions may seem unconventional or puzzling to some, this air of mystery is a deliberate aspect of their leadership style, serving to intrigue, inspire, and captivate those around them. Let's explore how the badass manager embraces their enigmatic nature to cultivate a sense of curiosity and wonder within their team.

1. **Cultivating Intrigue**: The badass manager understands the power of intrigue in capturing the attention and imagination of their team members. They deliberately cultivate an air of mystery around themselves, leaving others curious to unravel the layers of their personality and leadership style. By keeping people guessing, they

create a sense of excitement and anticipation that keeps their team engaged and motivated to learn more.

2. **Inspiring Wonder**: Like a puzzle waiting to be solved, the enigmatic nature of the badass manager inspires wonder and curiosity in those around them. Team members are drawn to their mysterious persona, eager to uncover the secrets behind their success and the strategies they employ. By presenting themselves as a source of fascination and intrigue, they ignite a sense of wonder and awe that fuels motivation and creativity within their team.

3. **Encouraging Exploration**: The enigmatic nature of the badass manager encourages exploration and discovery among their team members. Rather than providing all the answers upfront, they encourage individuals to embark on their own journey of self-discovery and exploration. By fostering a culture of curiosity and experimentation, they empower their team to think critically, challenge

assumptions, and uncover innovative solutions to complex problems.

4. **Fostering Connection**: While the badass manager may seem enigmatic and mysterious on the surface, they're also deeply attuned to the needs and aspirations of their team members. They use their mysterious persona as a means of drawing people in and fostering deeper connections based on mutual respect and admiration. Despite their air of mystery, they remain approachable and accessible, creating a sense of trust and camaraderie that strengthens team dynamics.

5. **Embracing Authenticity**: Beneath their enigmatic exterior, the badass manager remains authentic and true to themselves. They don't strive to be mysterious for the sake of it, but rather as a reflection of their unique personality and leadership style. While they may enjoy keeping people guessing, they're always transparent and honest in their interactions, earning the respect and trust of their team through their authenticity and integrity.

In conclusion, the enigmatic nature of the badass manager serves as a source of inspiration, intrigue, and wonder within their team. By cultivating intrigue, inspiring wonder, encouraging exploration, fostering connection, and embracing authenticity, they create a dynamic and engaging work environment where individuals are motivated to learn, grow, and push the boundaries of what's possible. Through their enigmatic leadership style, they inspire their team to embrace curiosity, think outside the box, and embark on a journey of continuous discovery and self-improvement.

Chapter 30: Zen and the Art of Badassery: The Manager's Path to Unwavering Resolve

In the whirlwind of leadership chaos, the badass manager stands as a pillar of inner strength and authentic confidence. They navigate challenges with grace and poise, relying not on trendy techniques but on their inherent badassery. Let's explore how the badass manager maintains their cool without relying on superficial practices, while still acknowledging the value of mindfulness and spirituality.

1. **Embracing Self-Assurance**: The badass manager exudes self-assurance without the need for flashy affirmations or pseudo-mindful exercises. They know who they are and what they're capable of, drawing strength from their inner resolve and authenticity. Their confidence isn't manufactured – it's rooted in a deep sense of self-awareness and respect for their own capabilities.

2. **Respecting Mindfulness**: While they may not engage in popular mindfulness practices, the badass manager respects the value of being present and attentive in every moment. They understand the importance of staying grounded and focused amidst the chaos of leadership, finding moments of clarity and reflection in the midst of the storm. While they may not meditate on a mountaintop, they find peace and centring in their own way.

3. **Honouring Inner Peace**: The badass manager values inner peace as a foundation for navigating the challenges of leadership with integrity and grace. They cultivate a sense of calm amidst the chaos, drawing on their inner reserves of strength and resilience to weather any storm. While they may not chant mantras or practice yoga, they find solace and tranquillity in moments of quiet reflection and introspection.

4. **Recognizing Authenticity**: Authenticity is the cornerstone of the badass manager's leadership style.

They lead with integrity and honesty, earning the respect and trust of their team through their genuine approach to leadership. While they may not preach omnipresent gratitude or senseless positivity, they lead by example, inspiring others to embrace their true selves and lead with authenticity.

5. **Nurturing Genuine Connections**: The badass manager values genuine connections and meaningful relationships, fostering a sense of camaraderie and trust within their team. They prioritize open communication and mutual respect, creating an environment where individuals feel valued and supported. While they may not engage in all team-building exercises or networking events, they prioritize meaningful connections that transcend superficial interactions.

In conclusion, the badass manager embodies inner strength and authentic confidence, navigating the challenges of leadership with grace and integrity. While they may not subscribe to traditional or popular mindfulness practices or spiritual techniques, they respect the value of staying grounded and centred amidst the chaos. By embracing their true selves and leading with authenticity, they inspire others to do the same, creating a culture of trust, respect, and resilience within their team.

Chapter 31: Embracing Curiosity: The Badass Manager's Quest for Originality

In the realm of leadership, the badass manager is fuelled by an insatiable curiosity and a relentless drive to explore the uncharted territories of innovation and originality. They understand that true greatness lies not in following the crowd, but in blazing their own trail and inspiring others to do the same. Let's delve into how the badass manager cultivates curiosity and champions originality within their team.

1. **The Quest for Knowledge**: The badass manager is a perpetual student of life, always hungry for new knowledge and insights. They encourage their team members to embrace a lifelong learning mindset, exploring new ideas, industries, and perspectives with curiosity and enthusiasm. By fostering a culture of intellectual curiosity, they empower individuals to expand their horizons and think outside the box.

2. **Embracing Diversity of Thought**: The badass manager recognizes that true innovation thrives in environments where diverse perspectives are welcomed and celebrated. They actively seek out input from individuals with different backgrounds, experiences, and viewpoints, valuing the richness and depth that diversity brings to the table. By embracing diversity of thought, they inspire their team to challenge conventional wisdom and explore unconventional solutions to complex problems.

3. **Encouraging Risk-Taking**: The badass manager understands that innovation requires a willingness to take risks and embrace failure as a stepping stone to success. They create a safe space for experimentation and exploration, encouraging individuals to push beyond their comfort zones and pursue bold ideas with confidence. By fostering a culture of calculated risk-taking, they embolden their team to embrace uncertainty and unleash their creative potential.

4. **Championing Originality**: The badass manager celebrates individuality and champions originality in all its forms. They encourage their team members to embrace their unique talents, perspectives, and ideas, empowering them to express themselves authentically and creatively. By fostering an environment where originality is valued and rewarded, they inspire individuals to dare to be different and strive for greatness on their own terms.

5. **Leading by Example**: Perhaps most importantly, the badass manager leads by example, as repeated multiple times in this book, embodying the spirit of curiosity and originality in their own actions and behaviours. They're not afraid to challenge the status quo, explore new frontiers, and pursue their passions with relentless determination. By leading with authenticity and conviction, they inspire others to follow their lead and unleash their own inner badassery.

In conclusion, the badass manager is a fearless champion of curiosity and originality, leading their team on a quest for greatness that knows no bounds. By embracing the unknown, celebrating diversity of thought, encouraging risk-taking, championing originality, and leading by example, they empower individuals to unleash their full creative potential and achieve extraordinary results. In the world of the badass manager, curiosity is king, and originality reigns supreme.

Chapter 32: Your Turn

Congratulations, you've made it to the final chapter, where the real fun begins! Now that you've soaked up all the insights from this book on how to be a badass manager, it's time to unleash your inner badassery and put your own spin on things.

Think of this as your opportunity to be the director of your own blockbuster movie, with you in the starring role as the badass manager extraordinaire. Take all the tips, tricks, and strategies you've learned, mix them up with your own unique style and flair, and watch as you create a masterpiece of leadership that's truly your own.

Remember, being a badass manager isn't about following a one-size-fits-all formula—it's about embracing your individuality, tapping into your strengths, and fearlessly blazing your own trail. So don't be afraid to shake things up, take risks, and dare to be different. After all, that's where the magic happens.

As you embark on this journey of self-discovery and badassery, keep in mind that greatness lies not in playing it safe, but in boldly stepping outside your comfort zone and embracing the unknown. So go ahead, embrace the challenge, embrace the chaos, and most importantly, embrace your own limitless potential.

So go forth, dear reader, and let your badass flag fly high. The world is waiting for your unique brand of awesomeness, and I have no doubt that you're destined for greatness. Now go out there and show 'em what you're made of.

Stay badass and never stop believing in yourself. You've got this.

Printed in Great Britain
by Amazon